Damien Lovelock grew up at Rose Bay and played rugby 'incessantly' until the age of 15. Then began a lifelong and life-threatening addiction to soccer. A careers adviser told him to become a photographer, a hairdresser or a psychiatrist; instead he did the next best thing and joined a rock band, the Celibate Rifles. Since 1980 he has recorded 11 albums with the Rifles, plus two solo albums. He has also met the Dalai Lama. He coached a women's soccer team in 1992 and does a soccer segment for Triple J radio station.

Damien has published one other book, *What's for Dinner, Dad?*, a cookbook for sole fathers, and writes for magazines like *Inside Sport, Underground Surf, Tracks*. He lives at Newport in Sydney with his son, Luke.

soccer

great moments,
great players
in world football

Damien Lovelock

A LITTLE
ARK
BOOK

ALLEN & UNWIN

First published 1996
A Little Ark Book
Allen & Unwin Pty Ltd
9 Atchison Street
St Leonards, NSW 2065, Australia
Phone: (61 2) 9901 4088
Fax: (61 2) 9906 2218
E-mail: 100252.103@compuserve.com

10 9 8 7 6 5 4 3 2 1

National Library of Australia
cataloguing-in-publication entry:

Lovelock, Damien.
    Soccer: great moments, great players in world football

    Bibliography.
    Includes index.
    ISBN 1 86448 085 8.

    1. Soccer — Australia — Juvenile literature. 2. Soccer — Juvenile
    literature. 3. Soccer for women — Australia — Juvenile
    literature. 4. Soccer for women — Juvenile literature. I. Title.
    (Series: True stories (St Leonards NSW)).

796.3340994

Photo credits
Cover photo: Sport. The Library (Darren Peacock)
Photo of 1974 Socceroos: the Fairfax Photo Library
All other photos from Sporting Pix, photographer Bob Thomas,
except for: 1993 Australian team (John Daniels), b/w of Pelé, Johan
Cruyff and Beckenbauer (all Popperfoto), women's World Cup 1991
(Bob Thomas/Joyner)
Photo research by Catherine O'Rourke

Designed and typeset by Mark Carter Design, Melbourne
Printed by McPherson's Printing Group, Maryborough, Australia

Contents

Acknowledgements

To Grandpa Fred, who played for Woolwich Arsenal
Gunners and tried unsuccessfully to introduce me to
soccer at age five;

to my mother, who convinced me at age 15 to try it;

to my father, who convinced me much later to take up
writing;

to Phil Wolanski and Robbie Szusz, my first coaches and
teammates at Vaucluse High;

to Lenny Glover, Allan Clarke, David Nish and John
Toshack, my earliest heroes;

to the 1974 Socceroos for giving us all that rarest of gifts, a
dream come true;

to Les Murray, Johnny Warren and Lou Gautier (Australian
soccer's Albert Einstein) for their invaluable and
generous assistance;

to Fiona Inglis for her priceless enthusiasm and support;

to Sarah Brenan, the newest and possibly most reluctant
soccer expert in the country;

to Triple J for being foolish enough to let me loose on
national radio;

to ABC-TV ditto;

to Luke, my son, for providing the incentive;

to Ann Scully for her ears;

to Edgecliff United, gone but not forgotten; and

to all the players in all the matches that I've enjoyed
so much

– thank you.

1 A game to remember

This is the kind of section that starts wars, breaks up marriages and makes the dog leave home. Anyone who says 'The greatest game of football was...' is asking for an argument. But I'll stick my neck out and nominate the second-round match between Belgium and USSR in the 1986 World Cup in Mexico as the all time-greatest game. If I had to show anybody one game of soccer to explain why I love the game so much, this would be the one.

After the first-round matches there was one team everybody was talking about, the USSR (Soviet Union). In the opening match they played Hungary, who had a good chance of making the semi-finals. The final score was 6-0 but it could have been 12-0. The Soviets went ballistic! In Belanov and Ratz they had two of the deadliest 25-metres-plus strikers in history. The Soviets scored from everywhere and played with such speed and precision that the Hungarians probably wished they hadn't qualified. The USSR team drew 1-1 with France (should have won), then beat Canada 2-0 at a walk. They were simply awesome.

The Belgians, on the other hand, were underwhelming to say the least. They began by losing 2-1 to Mexico, struggled to beat Iraq 2-1, then drew 2-2 with Paraguay. They had so little confidence that they hadn't even bothered to arrange hotel accommodation after the first round. Now they had to face the Soviets. Everyone, including the Belgians, thought it would be a one-sided match.

I was in Dublin with my band, the Celibate Rifles, at the time. I and six other guys were in a friend's lounge room struggling to find a position with a view of the TV that did not require an advanced knowledge of Hatha Yoga. (It was a very small room.)

The match began pretty much as expected. The USSR attacked the Belgians with frightening ferocity. It was as if they had at least three extra players on the field. Play swept from left to right and back again at unbelievable speed. The few times that a Belgian player was able to get the ball there was nobody to pass to, because the entire Belgian team was committed to last-ditch defence. Finally the inevitable happened – an Igor Belanov 25-metre special that shot into the goal like a Soviet surface-to-air missile. 1-0. The rest of the half continued in much the same way, the Soviets putting almost unbearable pressure on the Belgian defence, who time and again somehow managed to withstand the onslaught.

Half time arrived and everybody around me decided to hit the sack. They thought the result was a foregone conclusion. I thought that Belgium still had a chance. Counter-attacking football is based on letting your opponent do all the work and then punishing them with lightning-fast attacks as they begin to tire. Maybe the Belgians would do it this way in the second half.

The second half began where the first had left off, with a Belanov header hitting the post and then Vervoort

the Belgian fullback clearing off his own line. Then a subtle change began to creep over the game.

The Belgians began to do a little attacking of their own. The Soviets had dominated the midfield with their short passing game. Now the Belgians began to play the ball to the wings and then cross it back to the centre, looking for the head of their 186-cm captain, Jan Ceulemens.

Within two minutes they were rewarded as Enzo Scifo headed in a cross to level the scores. After one hour of almost total domination, the Soviets found themselves at 1-1 and faced with having to do it all over again.

Now both teams abandoned all pretence at tactics.

It was all-out attack. The battle raged from one end of
the field to the other, and while the Soviets still looked
awesome in attack they seemed vulnerable in defence,
especially against the high ball. Belgium, on the other
hand, seemed to get stronger as the game progressed.

For fifteen minutes both teams charged at each
other like Bengal Lancers. The tension and excitement
went right off the dial. Just as the possibility of a Belgian
victory began to seem slightly less absurd, Belanov
struck again. Running onto a through ball from Basily
Ratz, he placed his shot past keeper Pfaff with surgical
precision. It was 2-1 to the Soviets with 19 minutes
remaining.

> **The heat and the altitude of Mexico City had taken a tremendous toll.**

The heat and the altitude of Mexico
City had taken a tremendous toll on both
teams, but particularly the USSR. They were
exhausted. Their defence was leaden-footed
and their midfield had disappeared. They
decided to put on their two substitutes,
bringing on fresh legs to defend their lead.
This proved to be a huge blunder. It meant
they had no attacking players later when they
really needed them.

The Belgians again began chipping away at the
Soviet defence. Six minutes later Ceulemens collected a
50-metre pass on the edge of the Soviet penalty box.
When he turned he found, to his utter astonishment, that
no Soviet defender was bothering to challenge him
(there were three that could have). Ceulemens took a
stride and then slotted away his shot. Score 2-2, 13
minutes remaining.

Most members of the Soviet team were reduced to

a walk, suffering extreme fatigue and oxygen deficit. The Belgians now looked metres faster and mentally much stronger. The Soviets hit the post. Then with two minutes remaining the Soviet keeper made the save of the match to deny Enzo Scifo a second goal with a point-blank header at the far post. Even Scifo applauded. Extra time.

As the players began the first period of extra time, the Belgians found themselves with two priceless advantages. First, they had not used either of their substitutes (which they now did). Second, they had twice come from behind to level the scores and so had a psychological edge over their exhausted and dispirited opponents.

The Soviets again rallied and attacked, but the Belgian defence held strong. Then in the seventh minute a Belgian counter-attack resulted in a corner kick. The Soviet defence stood and watched as yet another high cross sailed into the area, on to a Belgian head and into the Soviet goal. 3-2 to Belgium.

The Belgians sensed victory now and attacked in numbers. In less than a minute a cross went straight past five Soviet defenders to Ceulemens on the left wing. He trapped the ball, turned, stopped and then accelerated, leaving his marker for dead. He crossed to Nico Clausens, who volleyed the ball past the keeper and into the net. Score 4-2 to Belgium.

With nothing to lose, the Soviets threw everybody forward. Crosses and shots rained on the Belgian goal, but keeper Pfaff and his band of faithful defenders scrambled them away. Belanov flung himself at a cross, missed, and landed heavily on the ground. The referee awarded a

penalty for a push in the back by a Belgian defender.
Belanov scored: 4-3 to Belgium, nine minutes to go.

Those nine minutes were the most exhausting I've
ever endured as a spectator – but also the most
exhilarating. And then it was all over and Belgium had
won, in one of the greatest upsets of the modern era.

DID YOU KNOW?

- An estimated 31.2 billion people watched the 1994
  World Cup finals tournament. This is roughly double
  the size of the next biggest TV audience, 15 billion for
  the 1992 Barcelona Olympics. (Both figures are total
  audiences over several weeks.)
- Over 180 countries entered the World Cup in 1994.
  This was eventually reduced to 24 teams, who
  contested the finals.
- FIFA has 178 member nations, making it bigger than
  the United Nations. The list ranges from Afghanistan to
  Zimbabwe.

---

2 History: from juggling judge to World Cup

One of the earliest versions of football that we know of was played in China at least 2000 years ago – we have

proof of it in a tomb uncovered in a remote part of China several years ago. The tomb belonged to a man called Ju Chong, a judge who was renowned for his skill at juggling a ball with his feet.

This was a game for a lone player. A variant of this early form of football is still practised by Shinto priests in Japan for ceremonies.

S O C C E R
History: from juggling
judge to World Cup

In Honduras in central America, archaeologists have discovered a version of football that was central to the religious worship of the people there. The losing team was decapitated (beheaded) – and their heads were used as the footballs for the next game. (This may explain the popularity of football as a spectator sport, the emphasis being on spectator!)

DID YOU KNOW?

- Balls used by the Pharaohs thousands of years ago were found in Egyptian graves. They were made of leather or linen and stuffed with reed or straw. Other early balls were made of skins sewn together, filled with earth, grain, corn husks or pieces of metal.

There is also evidence of this type of ritual in the hills of Afghanistan and many European and Scandinavian tribes would celebrate victory by using opponents' heads in games of post-battlefield footy.

When the Spanish conquistadors arrived in the Aztec Empire (Central America) in 1528, they found that the Indians there had refined the ancient game and were using a rubber ball, and goals as well. Again, a direct descendant of this, with only the hips used instead of heads and feet, can be seen today in a small area of north-western Mexico where it is played by the local *vaccheros* (cowboys).

The most direct forerunner of football as a *game,* however, can be traced back to the ancient empires of Greece and Rome around 2000 years ago. The game still flourished in the Italian city of Florence during the Middle Ages. It is still played in its original fifteenth-

century form once a year as part of a celebration of Florentine life.

And we know that in northern Europe, particularly Britain and France, football matches between villages became part of the tradition of country life. Goals were at either end of the village, and there could be over 500 players in a game lasting all day. Some of these games were so unruly and violent

Over 500 players in a game lasting all day.

S O C C E R
History: from juggling
judge to World Cup

that a number of English and Scottish kings tried to ban them. A royal edict mentioned 'a great noise in the city, caused by hustling over large balls'.

So, it seems that long long ago football was part of a ritual celebration of the winners over the losers on the battlefield.

Then we find football becoming part of the ritual of religious worship, in both Asia and South America.

Finally, in Europe and the 'new world' (the Americas) we see its development as a sport or recreation.

School rules

The modern game of football comes from English schools at the end of the 1700s.

Two crucial forms of the mob game emerged, one at the Harrow School, the other at the Rugby School. The 1830s Harrow game (still played by students of the school even now) was a dribbling, kicking affair that eventually became what we call soccer today. The Rugby version relied much more on handling and physical aggression.

Other schools had different rules again. The trouble was that when everyone finished school and went off to university, no two boys played the same game. This resulted in total chaos. Imagine trying to play a game that has soccer players, rugby players and volleyball players all on the field at the same time using the

DID YOU KNOW?

• When Sheffield played a village team, they sometimes gave the villagers a pair of white gloves and a silver coin to hold throughout the match, to stop them using their hands.

same ball but different rules!

Something had to be done. And it was, at Trinity College, Cambridge in 1848. Representatives from all the major football schools got together to decide on a set of rules. One of them said, 'I remember how the Eton men howled at the Rugby men for handling the ball'.

The Cambridge rules were quickly adopted and football clubs such as Sheffield and Wanderers were formed in the late 1850s. However, people still disagreed over some of the finer points of the game.

Finally a series of meetings was held in London in 1863 to decide whether the game should be a handling, running game (à la Rugby) or more of a dribbling, kicking game (à la Harrow).

At the fifth meeting two representatives from Harrow said that hacking (tripping or shin-kicking) and handling the ball should be banned. The two Blackheath members objected, but they were outvoted. They left the room in disgust, taking with them their handling, running code which would develop into rugby football.

Those who remained formed the Football Association, with the first official set of rules. And thus the modern game of soccer was founded.

Global spread

Soccer was especially popular with the middle classes and factory workers in the north of England. Here many football clubs were founded in the 1860s. The FA or

Football Association cup was established in 1871.

By the mid-1870s the game was spreading around the world at an astonishing rate, due largely to the movement of British migrants all over the globe.

In May 1904 a meeting was held in Paris to establish a world governing body, the Fédération Internationale de Football Association, or FIFA. FIFA remains the controlling body of world football to this day.

Football was included as part of the Olympic Games in 1900.

Jules Rimet, a French lawyer, became president of FIFA in 1921. He decided that a world football tournament (other than the Olympics) should be held. In 1930 the first World Cup finals were held in Uruguay.

DID YOU KNOW?
- The original World Cup trophy (the Jules Rimet trophy) was hidden during World War II and then stolen in 1966 from a display in England. It was found by a dog named Pickles under a garden hedge. After winning three World Cups, Brazil was allowed to keep it – but it was stolen again, from a display case in Rio de Janeiro. The thief later confessed he had melted it down.

---

3 Placing the players: from Pyramid to Penguin

Football (or soccer) is fundamentally a simple game. It's about scoring more goals than your opponent. Pretty basic stuff really...Right. So how do we do this?

To answer this question we need to think about tactics and strategy. The key is to get a perfect balance between attack and defence. If you have too many players in attack, then you will have an inadequate defence. The reverse is also true (just ask anyone who watched the Sweden versus Brazil semi-final in the 1994 World Cup).

To understand the present formations, let's go back to England around 1850 and see what was happening then.

Early days

A soccer match in the 1850s was like an under-7s game in the local park. Players were strung across the field, with perhaps two of them committed to defence. This was quickly abandoned in favour of something like a 'ruck' or rolling maul, where all players move together in the same direction, as seen in present-day Rugby Union.

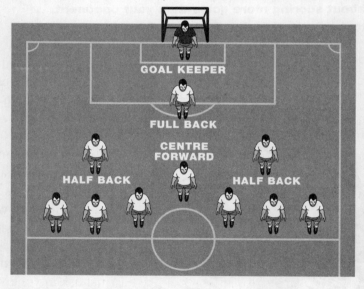

Standard formation 1850-70

This game was a bit like trench warfare. Players stood in two lines facing each other, about 10 metres apart – then they charged. The major problem with this was that teamwork was virtually impossible (the players were too close together to pass to each other effectively) and there was no depth in defence or attack.

The first big development was during the years 1870-80. The Scottish national team began playing England regularly using the following system.

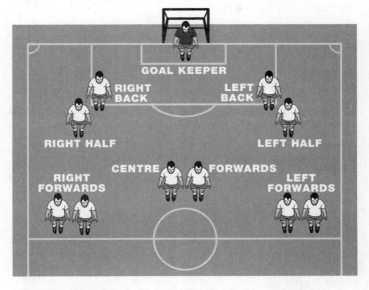

Scottish 'pairing and passing' system, 1870-80

It proved to be an overwhelming success because it promoted inter-passing and team play rather than the skills of each individual player.

Scotland brought the revolutionary 'pairing and passing' system to England in 1872. (Players moved down the field in twos, and the one that had the ball would pass to his pair as they came up to the opposition fullback.) The result was a draw. However, in the next 15

years England managed only one victory and suffered
defeats of 7-2, 6-1, 5-1. A tactical success for Scotland!

In response to this, the English developed the 2-3-5
or Pyramid system. It was very popular with fans and
players alike, as it made the game far more open and
interesting. It was so successful, in fact, that it was used
for the next 40 years.

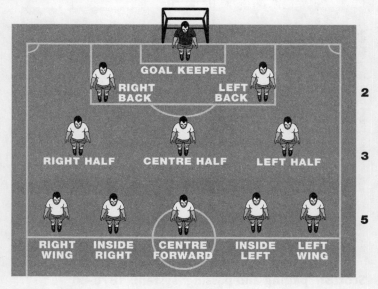

The 2-3-5 Pyramid 1880-1925

There was more space for each player, and scope
for a 'second phase' or midfield (the three halves) to
attack as well as the forwards. The key player in this
formation was the centre half. He attacked and defended,
as his two colleagues did, and could choose to pass to the
right or left or send the ball a long way forward. The
fullbacks guarded the area in front of the goal.

Winning in the midfield

The next major change was in 1925 and was probably brought in by Herbert Chapman, manager of Arsenal. The 'offside rule' had been changed so that there only had to be two players between an attacker and the goal instead of three. This meant that using the offside trap as a defensive philosophy was far more risky. Chapman's response was to dream up the WM formation.

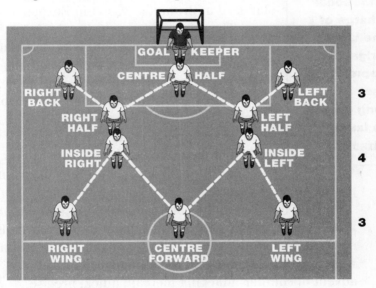

WM formation 1925-45 (dotted lines show W and M).
It sometimes changed from 3-4-3 (as shown) to 3-3-4 (only
one inside forward dropping back to be with the two halves)

You can see in the diagram that the centre half has become a centre back, or stopper – a defender – in the middle of the W. His job was to 'mark' (or 'mind') the opposing centre forward. The inside forwards now

23

directed or controlled the attack – the midfield
dominated the game. From now on, virtually all UK
matches would be won and lost in this crucial area.

Because of Herbert Chapman's system,
Arsenal dominated League and Cup football
for several years, establishing a reputation
that survives to this day.

While the WM formation was the
standard in Britain, it wasn't in Europe.

> **The English
> preferred the
> more
> 'emotional'
> Charge of
> the Light
> Brigade
> approach –
> they used
> long passes
> to launch
> attacks.**

The Austrians were using the 2-3-5
system (the old Pyramid) but with one major
difference. The Austrians, the Hungarians
and the Czechs used a short passing game.
Their emphasis was on skill and control, on
keeping the ball as close to the ground as
possible – 'on the carpet'. The English
preferred the more 'emotional' Charge of
the Light Brigade approach – they used long
passes to launch attacks.

The Italians used a combination of the WM and the
2-3-5 system. At the 1930 World Cup an Italian journalist
remarked 'the other team does all the attacking, but Italy
wins the game'. And it did, all of them. This was the
advent of counter-attacking football; quick, precise,
deadly. The Italians still use it today.

Meanwhile, the South Americans still favoured the
2-3-5 system with the emphasis on attack. Simple, huh?

Superman without a cape

Now, with all this knowledge at our fingertips, we move
on to Hungary, home of goulash, rhapsodies and some
guy named Jack (Hungary Jack...get it?) and another guy

named Gustav Sebes, the Hungarian national coach.

Ever since Herbert Chapman had turned the centre half into a centre back the job description for a centre forward had changed from *'elusive, with good dribbling and heading skills, clean, non-smoker'* to something like *'must be 195 cm, 104 kg (6'6", 16 stone), able to run for 90 minutes; should enjoy physical pain and have very little regard for personal safety'*. In other words, you needed Superman without a cape.

To the dismay of Gustav Sebes and many other people, in the 1950s there were no capeless Supermen centre forwards anywhere...not a one. To solve this dilemma, Sebes came up with the following formation, based around the 'deep-lying centre forward'.

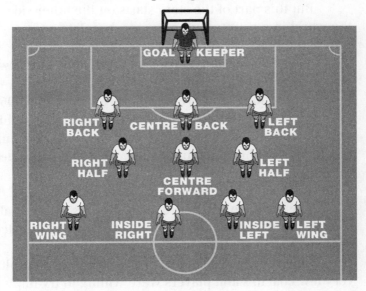

The Hungarian system 1945-55, using the 'deep-lying' centre forward (Hidegkuti)

(Actually Hidegkuti, the number 9, was not a centre forward at all, but an attacking centre half.)

Sebes inverted the M and turned it into a W in attack (making WW). The main point of this change was that it caused a dilemma for the opposition centre back. If he came forward to mark Hidegkuti, he left a huge gap in front of goal. If he stayed in position, then Hidegkuti simply cut the opposition to pieces with his passing game...Beautiful.

The strange case of the Swiss Bolt

At the same time as Gustav Sebes was perfecting his system, another tactical change was under way in Uruguay. It inspired one of the most exciting periods in world football, the Golden Age of Brazil.

But this part of the story starts on the other side of the world in a country full of snow, chocolate and numbered bank accounts...Switzerland.

Now 'Switzerland' and 'soccer' are not exactly two words that combine in most people's minds with the force of, say, 'long' and 'weekend'. However, at the 1950 World Cup tournament, an unheard-of system from this little-known country produced two of the most amazing results in World Cup football. The coach who concocted this 'miracle in the Alps' was Karl Rappan, and his system was called the *verrou,* or Swiss bolt.

The Swiss bolt required all 10 players to travel all over the field, changing from attack to defence and vice versa with alarming speed. The extreme fitness requirements were its biggest problem and, as a result, very few coaches and players were willing to try it.

You can see the advanced position of the midfield, especially the centre half, in attack.

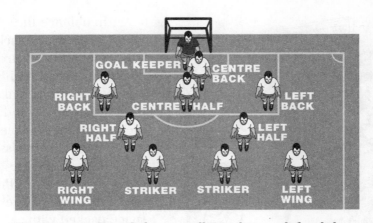

The Swiss Bolt in defence – all 11 players defend deep in their own territory. The centre back slides back deepest of all

The Swiss Bolt in attack – basically this is a 3-3-4 pattern, with an attacking centre half

In defence the whole team drops back. The 'stopper' or centre back goes deep into his own penalty area, sliding back and forth behind the last line of defence; hence the name 'Swiss bolt'. You can see the crowding in front of the goal, with all the 'free' space packed with defenders.

This approach to football later resurfaced in Italy as a system known as *Catenaccio*.

The Golden Age of Brazil: attacking fullbacks

In the 1860s the English played soccer with One fullback
In 1872 the Scots increased it to Two
In 1925 Herbert Chapman and Arsenal upped it to Three
In 1950 the Hungarians made it Three and a half
In 1958 the Brazilians made it Four

In the 1950 World Cup final, Uruguay used four defenders in a 'Swiss bolt' approach, and beat Brazil. The Brazilians, after recovering from the shock, decided 'never again'. They came up with a 4-2-4 pattern. As we have already seen, coaches and players had been experimenting with this idea, but it usually involved having a midfielder drop back to defend, as in the

Hungarian system and the Swiss bolt. The Brazilians did it differently – they had an extra fullback (sometimes two) who could be used in both attack and defence. Carumba!

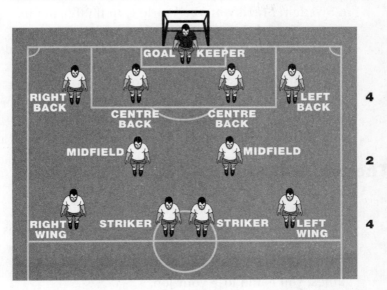

Brazil's version of 4-2-4, used in 1958. In attack, one or two of the fullbacks moved forward, changing the pattern to 3-3-4 or even 2-4-4. In defence, the left wing dropped back into midfield, giving a 4-3-3 formation

To make it work you needed really fit fullbacks with dribbling and passing skills and the ability to shoot. The attack-minded Brazil had these, and used as many as eight players forward at one time.

If this system had any weakness, it was in defence. Three players in the midfield is dangerously few – especially when everyone else was putting a new focus on defence and close marking in soccer.

Hungary reached the 1954 World Cup final using its version of 4-2-4, and only a tremendous injury toll from earlier games prevented it from winning. In 1958, in Sweden, Brazil won the World Cup final using its more refined 4-2-4 system, as shown in the diagram. (A new 17-year-old forward named Pelé had a bit to do with the team's success as well.)

After the shock results in 1950 when Uruguay beat Brazil using the Swiss bolt, and again in 1954 when a dour West Germany beat a badly injured Hungary, it was re-assuring to know that the best team had won the World Cup.

The big rethink

Following the 1958 World Cup, a big rethink began sweeping through world soccer. Television had something to do with it. Suddenly players and coaches were in the limelight – and if they put on a poor show, TV stations lost money. If your team lost too many games, you could lose your job.

Coaches realised that they could not 'out-attack' the Brazilians, especially with superstar players like Pelé in the team. *Not losing* became the focus! Winning was something you thought about after you'd made sure of not losing.

The 1962 World Cup was the first example of this new ideology. Even Brazil showed up using a 4-3-3 system. Outrageously skilled individuals like Pelé, Puskas (Hungary) and Garrincha (Brazil) were now seen

> **DID YOU KNOW?**
> * The English won the World Cup in 1966 with a formation called the Penguin, so-called because it was wingless.

as assets only if they could be coached and disciplined into a 4-3-3 strategy or the like. An undisciplined player was an unwanted player.

The 4-3-3 system used in the 1960s. Brazil won a World Cup in 1962 with this system and England did it again four years later (well, sort of). The winger can be on right or left

Goals are the proof of any system. Here is a table showing the average goals per World Cup game in 1954, 1958 and 1962. The lower scores reflect the trend towards defensive soccer.

	Goals	Games	Average
1954	140	26	5.38
1958	126	35	3.60
1962	89	32	2.78

The Dark Ages of world football

If the coming of the 4-3-3 system can be seen as storm clouds over the horizon, then what was going on in Italy at the same time was 'the Dark Ages' of world football. The Italians had seized upon the 'Swiss bolt' system, discarded after the 1950 World Cup finals and now completely forgotten by everyone except them.

By the early 1960s they had perfected the bolt system, developing it into the *Catenaccio* (which literally means 'the chain'). By 1970, this word was hated by soccer fans around the world. It was associated with everything negative and destructive in modern football.

As with the 4-3-3 and the Swiss bolt itself, *Catenaccio* was designed to *not lose* games rather than to win them. It began as 1-3-3-3, turned into 1-4-3-2 and at its peak (or rather depth) was 1-4-4-1.

The key man was the *libero* or sweeper. He patrolled the area behind the defensive backs, all of whom played tight man-to-man marking games. He sealed any gaps that remained. The idea was to strangle the opposition's offence, relying on lightning-fast counter-attacks to score a goal. After scoring

> **The idea was to strangle the opposition's offence, relying on lightning-fast counter-attacks to score a goal.**

you went back into defensive mode and stayed there until the game ended. A score of 1-0 became a common result in Italian first division.

Catenaccio was certainly effective – it did make scoring extremely difficult for the other sides. But as a philosophy it was about as popular as a fart in a space suit. It just stank, big time. And it buried the talents of some of the most gifted players Italy has ever produced.

In 1970 when Brazil, using a kind of 4-4-2 system, played Italy using a 'super-*Catenaccio*' formation of 1-4-4-1, soccer had turned itself completely inside out. What had once been a joyous attacking game dominated by supremely skilled individuals had now become a boring corporate enterprise where the point was not losing rather than winning. Individualists were seen as liabilities rather than assets, and the fans, especially in Italy, had been largely forgotten.

Could things get any worse? Most fans were afraid to ask.

Then, just when things were at their most bleak, the most extraordinary thing happened! But before I tell you what it was, let us jump back in the time machine and go back to 1955 when an Austrian man named Willy Meisl wrote a book called *Soccer Revolution*. In that book, he says that soccer teams should look for all-rounders – players who can do anything. 'A fullback seeing an opening in front of him must seize his chance without hesitation. A winghalf or winger will fall back, if necessary, and being an all-rounder will not feel out of place.' In other words defenders will attack, attackers will defend and it will all happen at alarming speed. It would be a *blitzkreig* that could come from anywhere at any time. In fact, it came from Holland.

Total football

Holland up to 1970 had had a long but unremarkable history in world football. Then in 1970 a Dutch club called Feyenoord won the European Cup. Far out. Then in 1971, again in 1972 and still again in 1973, Ajax, another Dutch club, won the European Cup. Something was definitely happening in Tulip Town. The something was 'total football' and the someone who made it happen was a player called Johan Cruyff (helped by a coach called Kovac). It arrived just in time to save the game from being strangled to death by defence-obsessed coaches.

The Dutch seemed to have taken the idea of the Swiss bolt inventor Karl Rappan 'that the team should outnumber its opposition in attack

Something was definitely happening in Tulip Town.

and defence' and combined it with the best aspects of Brazilian fluidity and rhythm in attack. The result was a kaleidoscope of movement, dazzling to watch and impossible to defend against.

Franz Beckenbauer, the German *libero supremo,* said in an interview that the reason total football scared opponents and coaches to death was because they looked for the secret pattern and couldn't find it. In fact there was no pattern. Everything was made up on the spot!! Brilliant.

Total football was the last great innovation in tactics and strategy. Anyone who saw the Dutch national team (with Cruyff as captain) between 1970 and 1974 will never forget it.

> **...opponents and coaches looked for the secret pattern**

In the lead-up to the World Cup final in 1974, Holland won seven games, scoring 14 goals and conceding just 1. However, they fell at the final hurdle, just as Hungary had 20 years earlier, being beaten 2-1 in the final by West Germany.

Cruyff retired from international football after the 1974 finals, and total football, in its purest form, disappeared almost as magically as it had arrived just four years before.

And that's pretty much the whole enchilada on football strategy and tactics. Throughout the 1970s, 1980s and 1990s tactical changes have come and gone. The key to today's game seems to be patterns that allow for on-the-spot decisions and a whole lot of players in the midfield. This history will hopefully allow you to watch soccer with a deeper understanding of the way the game is played. Watch TV matches and see if you can pick the patterns of play.

'Not the good old days': stamina vs skill

Before Karl Rappan invented his Swiss Bolt everyone still assumed that the number 1 requirement for playing high-level soccer was skill. With the Bolt, all that changed. Very fit players could play the system even if they weren't as skilful – but very skilful players could not play it unless they were also super-fit. Hence the emphasis is more on stamina than skill.

This approach really caught on in England – the 1966 World Cup tournament was won by an English side described as courageous, selfless, hard-working, honest ... in fact, everything except skilful and intelligent. The English had taken a 4-3-3 system and turned it into 4-1-3-2. In effect they had five fullbacks – the complete reverse of the pinnacle of attacking soccer, the 2-3-5 pyramid!

George Best, possibly the most gifted British player of all time, said, 'Stamina's all right, you've got to be able to run but you've also got to be able to do the main thing: to know what to do with the bloody ball! At its simplest level that's what's wrong with British football today...too many people who can run all day but can't kick a ball!'.

Foul! – or football and Jack the Ripper

Another development that arrived big time during the 1966 World Cup was the 'tactical foul'. This is like calling Jack the Ripper a nice chap with a rather unfortunate habit. What it meant was methodically kicking the great players out of the game. In 1966 the Bulgarians and the Portuguese did it to Pelé. By 1970 everyone had done it to George Best.

Fouling great players wasn't new. There'd been legendary violent matches all through soccer's history...look at the Battle of Bern in 1954 (Hungary versus Brazil...43 free kicks, two penalties awarded, four cautions, three send -ffs and an all-in brawl in the dressing room afterwards...not bad for two of the most attacking teams in history!) Here was an event fuelled by passion that turned into frustration and then violence.

However, the tactical foul had nothing to do with passion or hot-headedness. Quite the contrary, it was often a basic part of the tactics of a defensive team. A specific player would be given the job of 'hacking' the opponents' star forward out of the game. Ahh...the good old days.

> **A specific player would be given the job of 'hacking' the opponents' star forward out of the game.**

As this idea took hold, which it did rather like a bushfire in a national park, another funny thing happened... nothing.

> **By 1970 most attacking or creative players in world football realised that they could not expect much protection from referees**

For nearly 20 years this attitude was allowed to flourish unchecked by referees and other officials. Not only that, it was often justified and condoned by the media. (Example: Maradona was crippled because he was too talented.)

By 1970 most attacking or creative players in world football realised that they could not expect much protection from referees against 'hard' marking. They might get a free kick, the opponent a caution, very occasionally a send-off – but usually it was just 'play on'. To protect themselves, these players began to exaggerate, to ham it up, when they were fouled by opponents.

It worked. Free kicks began flowing, clumsy-footed defenders began to concede penalties. By the 1980s 'diving' was the most popular innovation in attacking football since the game began! Attacking players, having broken into the clear, would often slow down to allow the defence to catch up to them just as they reached the penalty area. Then they would dive as though they had been

It's our new strike weapon

viciously hacked down...Penalty! In fact slow-motion replays often revealed they hadn't even been touched. West Germany actually won the 1990 World Cup with a dive against Argentina. Some called it poetic justice. Most just said 'Enough!'

Away from the firing line

In the 1990s we see less and less of the old tactics and positions.. Wingers have gone, centre forwards also. Teams like Argentina and Italy play with one forward at most and he is almost certainly not the most creative player or main striker in the team. These you will find in the midfield (along with almost everybody else!).

As defences have become bigger, fitter, faster and more cynical the best players have faced the choice: either be systematically strangled, or keep away from the firing line. Maradona, Guillet Baggio, Michel Platini and countless others have done just that. As a result, the midfield has become so overpopulated that sometimes it looks more like the electrical appliance department during the July sale than a football field.

The emphasis on defensive soccer, team strategies and stamina in some countries devalues the gifted individual. A recent example is Glen Hoddle of Spurs and England fame, now player/manager of Chelsea. He was

---

DID YOU KNOW?
• Referee Sergio Vasquez of Chile was fined and suspended in 1975 following a match between Chile and Uruguay in Santiago during which he sent off 19 players. (Not bad considering you only get 22 to begin with!)

beautifully balanced, with great vision, creative passing, and an excellent free kick-taker. In fact, he was one of the few British players in the 1980s to command the respect of foreign media and managers alike – at a time when English football was really in the S-bends. Yet Hoddle could never get a permanent place in the English team. When he was included he had to change his natural style so much that he looked constantly uncomfortable, and therefore underconfident. In most European or South American countries he'd have been made captain, hailed as a genius and retired as a national monument selling razor blades and health insurance.

DID YOU KNOW?

- Zaire was the first black African country to reach the World Cup finals, in 1974. The country's president promised each squad member a house, car and family holiday. The team lost three games, didn't score a goal and gave away 14 goals. The offer was withdrawn.
- Barcelona has a whole floor of its club building set aside for soccer trophies and memorabilia.

---

4 High five: the all-time greats

Most sports writers agree that since 1966 there have been only five players who could truly be called geniuses: Pelé, George Best, Johan Cruyff, Franz Beckenbauer and Diego Maradona.

Technically they were all perfect. Control, passing, heading, shooting, the works. At their peak, they were all superbly fit athletes, beautifully balanced, graceful as gazelles, deadly as leopards. On top of that, each was gifted in a special way. I remember Pelé's anticipation, Best's almost magical ability to dribble and swerve at full speed, Beckenbauer's uncanny sense of when to inject himself into an attack, Cruyff's explosive acceleration and ability to 'read' a game and Maradona's ability to destroy a defence single-handed with a running and passing game of unequalled brilliance.

Pelé

Pelé began his career in the mid-1950s as a shy teenager and ended it in the late 1970s as the founder and patron saint of the ill-fated American Soccer League. Along the way he collected two World Cup final winners' medals, in 1958 and 1970, scored the most goals in history (over 1300) and was declared sports star of the twentieth century while there was still 30 years left of it. He was also labelled a national resource of Brazil (and therefore non-exportable). Not bad for kicking a ball around a park!

Pelé's real name was Edson Avantes do Nascimento, and he was born in the 'Three Hearts' district of the city of Santos, Brazil. The young Pelé's amazing skills were spotted while he was still playing barefoot street football, and he was invited to join the Bauru Club. Later he moved to Santos, which was his home club for almost his entire playing career. Despite reaching heights of wealth and acclaim that no other player has been able to equal, Pelé has never forgotten the poverty and hardship of his origins. His work for homeless and underprivileged children all over the world is legendary.

Word quickly spread of an outstanding new talent in Brazilian football, but it was not until the 1958 World Cup finals tournament in Sweden that most soccer fans and journalists saw what all the fuss was about.

To shine in the midst of such champions as Garrincha, Vava, Didi, Nilson Santos and Djalma Santos required a level of excellence that was well beyond most international players at the time. Pelé did it at age 17, culminating with two goals in the final. So Brazil discovered the greatest individual playing talent in history and finally won its first World Cup final all in the same year.

The 17-year-old Pelé already had complete ball control, perfect footwork and incredibly wide peripheral vision. Perhaps more than any of these marvellous gifts, the thing that made the entire soccer world take Pelé to heart was the spirit of sheer, exuberant joy with which he played the game. Scoring a goal in his third successful World Cup final in 1970, he still celebrated with the enthusiasm of a nine-year-old playing in his first season.

He had courage too. One of the enduring images of world football must surely be the sight of Pelé, his face contorted by pain and frustration, being carried from the field during the Brazil v. Portugal World Cup tie in 1966. The greatest player on Earth had been savagely and methodically kicked out of the match. Needless to say, with him went Brazil's hopes of victory. In those days no substitutes were allowed, so ten minutes later Pelé reappeared, legs a mass of bandages. Barely able to stand, he played out the remainder of the game. For some reason this is the picture that comes to my mind still when I hear the name Pelé.

In a first-class career of nearly 25 years Pelé scored 1363 goals, played 111 internationals scoring 97 goals, and helped his team win three World Cup finals. Along the way he became the best-known and best-loved popular figure in sport this century. At the twilight of his career he signed with the New York Cosmos, members of the fledgling North American Soccer league, and almost single-handedly popularised the sport in the USA. Since retiring he has become a tremendous ambassador for the game, as well as continuing his tireless efforts for the underprivileged children of the world. If that isn't enough, in 1994 he decided to take on the Brazilian FA to root out corruption in the game. Long live the King!

George Best

When it comes to scandals, public disgrace, tragedy and triumph in the daily press, there is one sports star who stands out like a beacon...George Best. If Diego Maradona, Paul Gascoigne, Eric Cantona and countless others have been victims of the nastiest kind of gutter journalism, George Best copped it first and worst. It was a whole new way to talk about a footballer. No one who followed football in the 1960s will ever forget him.

The late 1950s and early 1960s might have belonged to Brazil and Pelé, but from 1966 to 1970 George Best was the superstar. He was more of an individualist than Pelé. His greatest skill was his dribbling – the ability to beat opponents by performing a series of feints, swerves and dummies using both feet, the ball, his body, his eyes, whatever, and all at a full sprint. Added to this, he was a lethal shot with both feet and was an excellent header of the ball.

Off the field was another story. While Pelé was the statesman of modern football, Best was the rogue; the rascal.

Best, like Pelé, came from humble beginnings. He was born in Belfast, Ireland, on 22 May 1946. His father Dick worked in the shipyards.

> **While Pelé was the statesman of modern football, Best was the rogue; the rascal.**

One day in 1961, Manchester United's talent scout in Northern Ireland watched as his own son's team was annihilated by a tiny 15-year-old with the 'physique of a toothpick'. When he rang the boss of Manchester United, he didn't waste words: 'I think I've found a genius,' he said. How right he was. Best appeared in Manchester United's first-division side in 1964 and by the end of the season was a regular player. To fully understand the impact George Best had, we must remember that British football in the 1960s was dominated by the hard-running, high-workrate, all-purpose approach. Teams were very defensive, big on fitness, low on skill. Individually gifted players were considered a luxury.

At the same time, life in Britain was changing. Old ideas were being questioned and rejected. This youth revolution was led by pop singers like the Beatles, the Rolling Stones and the Animals – and Georgie Best. By 1966 the press had taken to calling him 'the fifth Beatle'. The theme song of the era was 'My Generation' by the Who. It was an anthem of frustration against the boring, suffocating lifestyle of Britain in the early 1960s, expressed in the line 'hope I die before I get old'. Although George Best's message was sent out on the football field, it was the same. Bugger the boredom, let's take some risks and have some fun!

In 1968 Manchester United won the European Cup final. Best's display was galvanising. In the same year he was voted 'European Footballer of the Year'. It seemed that George could do no wrong.

If Best was the greatest sensation in British football on the field, his impact off it was no less amazing. His face could be seen endorsing everything from eggs and milk to bargain holidays and motor cars. His earnings off the field were more than ten times his playing salary. He grew his hair long, he owned clothing boutiques and nightclubs, he loved fast cars and beautiful women. He was a swinger in every sense of the word.

To someone growing up in the 1990s, this may not seem particularly unusual – but when George was doing it in the late 1960s he was doing it for the first time. There had simply never been a sportsman like him. The golden age of English football owed almost everything to an Irishman!

Several sports journalists and many of George's teammates wondered aloud how long any player could keep up the pace. The answer was 'Not very long'.

> **People even brought terminally ill children to his house to see if George could cure them with his touch.**

George was besieged by the newspapers, agents wanting him to put his name on things, women wanting to sleep with him, women wanting to marry him, men wanting to buy him a drink, men wanting to fight him...People even brought terminally ill children to his house to see if George could cure them with his touch. Added to this was George's showbiz lifestyle, late nights, heavy drinking, the works.

It was in a League Cup tie with Manchester City in 1969 that the cracks began to appear for everyone to see. Best was booked for kicking the ball away after the referee awarded a free kick against United. Later, as he walked off the field, Best knocked the ball out of the referee's hands (this was on national TV). Charge: bringing the game into disrepute. Sentence: 14 weeks suspension.

His first game back was an FA Cup tie against Northampton. United won 8-0. Best scored six goals. A month later he was sent off for spitting and throwing mud at the referee while playing for Northern Ireland against Scotland. Sports journalists and fans called it a bad patch...but it was more than that. It was the beginning of the end.

> **'Georgie Best was made in heaven'**

George Best played 37 times for Northern Ireland, never appeared in a World Cup finals tournament, helped United win the League Cup twice in 1964-65 and again in 1966-67 and helped England win the European Cup in 1968. He was also voted European Player of the Year in 1968. He was United's leading scorer four times. George Best was, in my opinion, the most naturally gifted player since 1960.

In the early 1970s a new superstar came, in the form of Johan Cruyff. Best's teammate Derek Dougan said, 'Cruyff was manufactured on Earth. Georgie Best was made in heaven'.

Johan Cruyff

At the end of the 1960s, with George Best gone, things were looking pretty bleak for both fans and players of attacking soccer. Admittedly Brazil won the 1970 World Cup final with possibly the most perfectly balanced *jogo bonito* (beautiful game) side ever, featuring players like Pelé, Gerson, Jarzinho, Tostao, Rivellino and Carlos Alberto. Elsewhere it was a very different story. Coaches everywhere were falling over themselves to design new and more impenetrable eight-player defence systems.

Then a miracle happened. The miracle-bearer was a whippet-thin youngster with long hair, a hawkish face and an intense, passionate stare.

His name was Johan Cruyff and he was born one street away from the Ajax club stadium in Amsterdam. His widowed mother worked as a cleaner there. When Johan joined Ajax as a junior, the club helped her support her family. Again we see genius flowering in the most difficult and deprived conditions.

> **Again we see genius flowering in the most difficult and deprived conditions.**

In 1970, while Brazil was busy winning its third World Cup, a strange thing happened. A Dutch team won something! Feyenoord won the European Cup, the most prestigious trophy on the continent. A fluke, most people said...but over the next four years Holland showed how wrong they were.

In 1971 Ajax followed in Feyenoord's footsteps, winning the Dutch championship and then the European Cup. As a matter of fact, over the next four years there was precious little they didn't win. They were Dutch League champions 1970, 1972, 1973, Dutch Cup winners 1970, 1971, 1972, European Cup winners 1971, 1972, 1973, World Super Cup winners 1972, 1973, World Club champions 1972.

Meanwhile, Cruyff won the European Footballer of the Year award three times (1971, 1973 and 1974).

Cruyff was a player of extraordinary speed, balance, skill and intelligence. Where Best relied on his dribbling skills to defeat the close marking he was

Manchester United fan at the FA Carling premiership (Manchester United v. Coventry City)

Women's World Cup finals 1991, USA v. Japan

George Best, Manchester United

Below: Pelé is chaired from the match after the 1970 World Cup final (Brazil beat Italy 4-1)

Diego Maradona at the 1986 World Cup finals held in Mexico

Below: Franz Beckenbauer, captain of the winning West German side in the 1974 World Cup (West Germany defeated Holland 2-1)

Left: Beckenbauer's arch-rival, Johan Cruyff, celebrates a goal in a 1974 World Cup match

The 1974 Socceroos, including Johnny Warren — the first and only Australian team to get to the World Cup finals

Inset: Jimmy Mackay's boot (the one he used to kick *that* goal)

The 1993 Australian team won a World Cup qualifier against Canada 4-1 in a penalty shoot-out

subjected to, Cruyff used his ability to accelerate and change direction at unbelievable speed. He seemed to glide everywhere effortlessly, using a stop-start-stop-start change of pace and direction that baffled the best defences in the world. They simply had no answer.

And it wasn't just Cruyff. The entire Ajax team seemed to be playing some weird sort of musical chairs.

> **The entire Ajax team seemed to be playing some weird sort of musical chairs.**

Players appeared in defence, then in midfield, back in defence again but on the left instead of the right – and then Cruyff would explode down the wing, beating tackle after tackle...stop... and then deliver a perfect high cross. It would be headed into the net by Neeskens or Krol, who seemed to be playing both left back and right back as well as central midfield, but were in fact also playing the striker's role...if they felt like it. Forget tactics, positions, formations. In fact, throw the book away altogether.

We've already talked about 'total football'. Everyone did everything. Forwards defended, defenders attacked and everyone played midfield. The system relied on

> **Ajax players looked more like a rock band than a footy team.**

tremendous fitness and mental agility. But more than these, it relied on Johan Cruyff. He was the embodiment of the new ideal. Total attack...total awareness!

These new kids in town were a wild bunch. Although the 1960s had left an indelible mark on everything, professional football had remained pretty insulated from the revolution. Footballers grew their hair (a little) and grew moustaches (a lot) but otherwise they were just as they'd been for decades before that. Straight, with a capital S!

Ajax players, or 'the Flying Dutchmen' as they were called, looked more like a rock band than a footy team. They wore long hair, and love beads, were rumoured to smoke marijuana, believed that sex was the best preparation for a big match, and listened to rock music in the dressing room. Their style of play was wild, brilliant and free-spirited. Cruyff was always at the centre of it.

Cruyff was also establishing a reputation for bitter confrontations with coaches, trainers and managers. Holland was still an emerging country in professional football, and Cruyff was paid a lot less than he would have got in Italy, Spain or Germany. There were many well-publicised clashes.

In 1973 a bombshell was dropped that some Ajax Amsterdam fans have still not totally recovered from. Johan Cruyff and Johan Neeskens had been sold to Barcelona in Spain.

Cruyff's transfer fee was a world record £1 million (not far off $A2 million). In 1974 he and Neeskens returned to lead the Dutch World Cup challenge.

By now the whole football world was in a state nearing absolute panic about Cruyff and his fellow countrymen's brand of wizardry. Coaches were going blind watching slow-motion replays of the Dutch national team in action, searching for the secret behind 'total football'. But since there was no pattern to it, no one could find a formula to defeat it.

> **Coaches were going blind watching slow-motion replays of the Dutch national team in action.**

In the early rounds the Dutch didn't just beat their opponents, they thrashed them – first Uruguay, Sweden and Bulgaria; then Argentina, East Germany and Brazil. They scored 14 goals. They conceded just one. Their opponents in the final were the West Germans, the only other team with any claim to understanding total football.

The opening minute of the match remains one of the truly amazing stories of world soccer. Holland kicked off, passed the ball back through the midfield, seemingly doing nothing more than giving everyone a touch of the ball. Sixteen passes later, Cruyff collected the ball just inside the German half. He paused, then began tracking to the left, apparently aimlessly. Suddenly he darted forward, stopped, then darted again, losing his marker and was inside the German penalty area in a split second. The Germans seemed to be moving in slow motion. At the last second a trip brought him down. Penalty. Neeskens converted and Holland led 1-0 after less than 60 seconds. The Germans had not even touched the ball!

> **Holland led 1-0 after less than 60 seconds. The Germans had not even touched the ball!**

Germany went on to win the final 2-1. Defender Rudy Krol remarked afterwards, 'You can score too quickly...You start thinking about the result instead of the match. We thought we were world champions. We woke up too late'.

Cruyff returned to club football with Spanish first-division team Barcelona, and continued to enhance his reputation. In 1975 he joined Pelé, George Best and Franz Beckenbauer in the United States. He played a couple of seasons in Florida, then returned to Holland. Although Holland qualified for the 1978 World Cup finals, Cruyff didn't join the team. He had retired from international football.

He kept on playing at a lower level with Feyenoord and then with Ajax, finally retiring as a player in 1980. His record as a player was 48 internationals, producing 33 goals. In Dutch football he scored 215 league goals and in Spain he scored 47 with Barcelona.

He returned to Ajax in 1983 as a trainer and has gone on to become one of the leading coaches in Europe, winning titles with both Ajax and Barcelona. In 1994 his son made his debut with Barcelona. Cruyff was once asked if success as a coach made up for never collecting a winning finalist's medal in the World Cup. His answer was 'No,' followed by a brain-shrinking glare...'of course not!'

Franz Beckenbauer: *der Kaiser*!

Franz Beckenbauer was born in West Germany in 1945 at the end of World War II. Life in a country ravaged by six years of war was hard. Again, we see a brilliant sportsman growing up poor. (In interviews, Pelé, Best, Cruyff and Maradona all said that as children their only joy in life was a soccer ball.)

Beckenbauer first broke onto the world stage as a 21-year-old in the 1966 World Cup. West Germany battled into the final to meet England, the host nation. In one of the most dramatic and controversial games in history, England eventually won 4-2 in extra time. (A team of physicists has just proved conclusively that Geoff Hurst's decisive third goal was in fact not a goal. Hmmm...only took them 29 years.) Although he was on the losing team, Beckenbauer was quickly recognised as the new 'find' in world football. He dominated the game, reading and dictating changes in direction and style constantly. He had great speed and ball control, as well as a lethal right foot. Starting off as a classic midfielder he opted to drop further back into the defence and became the greatest sweeper (or *libero*) in history. Like the other genius players, Beckenbauer always appeared to have time when in possession of the ball.

In the 1970 World Cup Beckenbauer was again in the limelight, this time as Germany's captain. First he led Germany to an unforgettable victory over England in the quarter-finals. In the revenge match of the century, Beckenbauer inspired his team to a 3-2 victory after England had led 2-0 at half time. Then he led Germany into the semi-final against Italy, a team that was completely obsessed with ultra-defensive football. It was like the great wall of China, with eight players packed into the last third of the field. The key to victory for the Italians was to score first. They did and for the next

70 minutes the Germans, led by Beckenbauer, ground away at the most disciplined defence in football history.

In the second half Beckenbauer was heavily fouled. Instead of getting up, he lay on the ground, writhing in agony with a dislocated shoulder. He was carried from the field but he returned several minutes later with his right arm taped to his chest. The effect of his incredible display of courage was immediate. The Germans seemed suddenly to be fresher and faster than their opponents. Finally, in the 88th minute, Schnellinger equalised, 1-1. As the final whistle sounded Beckenbauer collapsed on the grass, his face grey with exhaustion and agony. Extra time. In the heat and the altitude of Mexico, this was almost torture.

...incredible display of courage

Germany scored first through Gerd Muller. 2-1. Italy, forced to attack in order to survive, equalised through fullback Burhnich. 2-2. Then Luigi Riva, Italy's lone attacker, scored with his cannon-like left foot. 3-2 to Italy.

With only minutes remaining, Beckenbauer launched a final attack. The Germans worked the ball downfield through the 11 Italian players and onto the head of Muller. 3-3. With two minutes to go, Giannini Rivera (who today is a member of the Italian parliament) scored directly from the kickoff to send Italy into the final and Germany to hell. Beckenbauer had again been on the losing side, yet he gave the world the greatest individual performance of the entire tournament.

In 1974 Franz finally got his winner's medal, defeating his rival Cruyff and the Flying Dutchmen. The

1970s proved to be a good period for Kaiser Franz all round. With Bayern Munich he achieved every honour in club football: league champions 1969, 1972, 1973, 1974, Cup winners 1969, 1971, European Cup winners 1974, 1975, 1976, World champions 1976. He was also twice voted European Player of the Year, in 1972 and 1976. He bowed out of international football and then in 1977 signed with the New York Cosmos. He finished his playing career with Hamburg in the early 1980s, retiring with the reputation of being West Germany's most complete footballer.

By going on to a second successful career as West Germany's coach, Beckenbauer achieved the unique distinction of competing in three World Cups as a player (1966, 1970 and 1974) and three as a manager (1986, 1990 and 1994), winning one of each.

Like Cruyff, he was dedicated, professional, but rather aloof. Perhaps these two players learned from the mistakes of George Best and others like him – they made sure their lives are quite separate from the game. While their attitudes to the press may at times ruffle a few feathers, their impact on world football cannot be denied. Both as players and later, as managers and coaches, they have proved their brilliance time and time again.

Maradona

If there was ever a player who had a precocious talent it was Diego Armando Maradona. His name, like George Best's, is synonymous with both genius and scandal. In the early 1980s he was Maradona, the God of Football: robust, athletic, mischievous, arrogant...astonishing. In the early 1990s he seemed more like a character from

'Heartbreak High' or 'Dallas' if Hunter S. Thompson wrote the script – bloated, miserable, drug-ravaged...here was excess with a capital E.

Diego Armando Maradona was born in Buenos Aires, Argentina in 1961. He played his junior football with a local team known as 'the Little Onions'. Even at age 10 the young Maradona showed a high level of skill as well as buckets of raw talent that marked him as a player of almost limitless potential. He was short but extremely strong, well-balanced and blisteringly fast. Almost exclusively left-footed, he was a magnificent striker of a dead ball as well as possessing a radar-like accuracy in passing. He played number 10 – the prize position —for his entire professional career.

> **He played his junior football with a local team known as 'the Little Onions'.**

By 1978 Maradona's achievements with Argentina's youth teams had alerted the sporting media that the new prince was in town and looking to get crowned as soon as possible! The same year he was selected in Argentina's World Cup squad. He was 17.

As training built up, the manager, Menotti, began cutting players to reduce the squad to a more manageable size. Then a bombshell. Maradona had been cut from the squad (he was in fact the last player to be dropped). Menotti announced to the world press that he had decided to hold Maradona back and give him more time to mature. Maradona left the training camp in tears...a sight that would unfortunately become all too familiar in later years.

All the same, the four-year-delay before the next World Cup proved a godsend for Maradona's career.

Clubs outside Argentina offered him astronomical sums. Finally, in 1982 he could resist no longer and went to Barcelona for £4.2 million (about $A7-8 million), a new world record.

It was definitely shaping up as a big year in Diego's life. The 1982 World Cup was to be held in Spain, and people's expectations were sky-high. The fact that Argentina was the defending champion seemed to have been forgotten. There was only one player that anyone cared about in the blue and white stripes – Maradona.

> **Belgium methodically butchered Maradona like a Sunday roast.**

The tournament, both for Argentina and Maradona, was a total disaster. In the first group match, Belgium methodically butchered Maradona like a Sunday roast (something which his shins bore a frightening resemblance to after the game). The referee did nothing. Argentina lost 1-0. Victories over Hungary and El Salvador got them to round 2, where they were grouped with Italy and Brazil. A tough draw for a number of reasons, one of them being Claudio Gentile the Italian defender, one of the most feared and ruthless backs in the game. Gentile tripped, kicked, elbowed and bumped Maradona so consistently and ferociously that he set a new record for fouls by one player on another in a single match (32!) After the game they didn't bother exchanging shirts – Gentile had already torn Maradona's off his back during the first half. Italy won 2-1. Again the referee did nothing.

In the next match, against Brazil, a bitter and frustrated Maradona lashed out against his opponents.

Now the referee acted! – and sent him off. He left the field in tears. Argentina lost 3-1.

His next two seasons at Barcelona proved to be very successful (domestic cup winners 1983, European Cup winners and cup champions in 1983), but after the Italians' triumph in the 1982 World Cup all eyes were on Italy's first division. And in 1984 that's where Maradona went, breaking his own world record with a transfer fee of £6.9 million.

Interestingly, though, he didn't follow the 'money trail' to the famous northern Italian clubs like Juventus, AC Milan and Inter Milan. Instead he opted for Napoli, a southern team with no track record in Italian football. This was a significant decision because the industrial north of Italy is much wealthier than the rural south. The fact that Maradona chose the peasants over the landlords instantly made him the most popular resident in Naples. During his eight turbulent seasons with Napoli, Maradona led them to great success (league champions 1987, 1990, cup winners 1987, UEFA cup winners 1989).

Before all that, however, came the 13th World Cup finals in 1986. With all eyes turned to Mexico, here, finally, was the perfect stage for Diego Maradona to show his genius.

Argentina began in Group I with Cup-holders Italy, Bulgaria and South Korea. Argentina looked shaky. It seemed to be a one-man team, with Maradona doing everything and doing it unsupported. It was almost as if his team-mates were as much in awe of his abilities as their opponents. They drew 1-1 with Italy due to a piece of Maradona brilliance, and progressed to Round 2 as group leaders.

Here they met the Uruguayans, the undisputed
butchers of South American football. (Their match with
Scotland looked like a Bruce Lee movie.) Maradona
chose this match to unleash his powers. He simply
mesmerised them. Although the score was only 1-0, the
outcome was never in doubt. The only question was
whether Diego's teammates could stay with him long
enough to reach the finals.

In the quarter-finals they drew England. It is this
match that is most closely associated with the legend of
Diego Maradona, for the best and worst reasons. The
game was a real tactical stalemate, the English
swarming in defence, the Argentines looking nervous,
unsure of whether to attack. Then Maradona collected
the ball outside the English penalty box, played a quick
one-two and leapt high above goalkeeper Shilton to head
the opening goal into the net. Great. Only one problem.
He headed the ball with his hand. Amidst tumultuous
scenes of protest from the English players and rapture

from the South American fans, Diego Maradona had done the unforgivable. He had cheated and got away with it.

The next goal was totally different. Collecting the ball in his own half, he spun, accelerated, swerved, dummied, changed pace and direction, accelerated again, dribbled, dummied and then held off a final challenge to beat Shilton again and score perhaps the greatest individual goal in World Cup history. He had run 60 metres past seven defenders and side-footed the ball into the net from one metre out. It was a breathtaking moment. Maradona 2, England 1.

> **He had run 60 metres past seven defenders and side-footed the ball into the net from one metre out. It was a breathtaking moment.**

In the semi-final, Maradona went through the Belgian defence like a wind-up toy gone berserk. Maradona 2, Belgium 0. In the final he led Argentina to a 3-2 victory over Germany. The myth was now complete. He was the greatest player in the world.

But, oh how quickly things can change. By World Cup 1990 the figure that led Argentina out onto the field bore little resemblance to the pocket-sized human dynamo who had seemed so utterly irresistible in Mexico. In his place was a bloated, lame and in fact rather sad little man. Maradona limped through the tournament on a badly swollen left knee. Argentina somehow survived long enough to make the final, then lost to Germany.

Maradona announced that he no longer wished to play in Italy. The constant attention of the press, the scandals (whether real or invented) and the endless demands of the adoring Napoli fans had taken their toll. Like George Best he had simply had enough. He just wasn't interested in the grind of training, fitness and matches any more. However, he still had a contract with Napoli, who said flatly that they would not release him. Then the first drug scandal occurred and Maradona found himself on his way to Seville in Spain.

In the next three years (1992-94) Maradona was...expelled from football for breach of contract, in court for shooting at newspaper reporters, charged with drug trafficking and being an employer of prostitutes, suspended from football for a positive drug test...etc., etc., etc. It was like a remake of the George Best story word for word. Was it true? Some of it, probably.

Without Maradona at the helm, Argentina struggled in the lead-up to the World Cup 1994. After being thrashed by Colombia in Buenos Aires, the Argentines were forced to qualify through the repercharge play-off. In this case their opponents were none other than Australia. In a desperate bid to avoid utter public disgrace, the Argentine management approached Maradona to try and coax him out of retirement for one final campaign. Rumours flew through the football world. Yes he would, no he wouldn't, he's injured, he's too old... Finally, two weeks before the Sydney match, it was confirmed. Maradona was in training in an attempt to shed a lot of kilos and get somewhere near match fitness. The guy was 33 years old and had played one and a half seasons of real football in four years!

Australia did a more than half-decent job, with a 1-1 draw. Argentina got its goal because of one moment of Maradona genius – a pass hit so perfectly that it virtually led the player to the ball to score with a header. The return in Argentina was a hometown triumph.

The 1994 finals were held in the USA. In the early games the Argentines blew their opponents away with inspired attacking football. When they came forward they seemed to come from everywhere, and their finishing was absolutely lethal. And at the heart of it all was Maradona, grinning like a maniac and generally having the time of his life. People began to believe that yes, the miracle might just happen.

> **...at the heart of it all was Maradona, grinning like a maniac and generally having the time of his life.**

Then, almost on cue, the big scandal exploded. Maradona was tested for drugs and the result was positive. The next day he was expelled. The impossible dream had been blown apart. It was bitterly disappointing.

> **STOP PRESS:**
> • November 1995...He's back! – playing club football for Boca Juniors in his beloved Argentina and excelling in his new role as anti-drug campaigner. Stay tuned for the next exciting episode.

5 Socceroos and Olyroos: soccer in Australia

Australia has a reputation as a sporting nation (a sports-mad nation?). For a country that is so isolated and has so few people, our success in world competition is extraordinary – in cricket, athletics, tennis, swimming, surfing, motor racing, horse racing, Rugby league, Rugby union and golf. So why are we not even contenders in the world's most popular game?

A Cinderella sport

There's one fairly simple answer. In Europe, South America, Asia and Africa there is only one winter sport...soccer. In Australia we have four codes: soccer, which is truly international; rugby (League and Union), which is played in a few countries; and AFL or Australian Rules, which is played exactly nowhere else. In terms of spectator popularity at the highest level AFL comes in first, Rugby League second, Rugby Union third and soccer fourth. Soccer is *the* game in many countries. Here it's a Cinderella sport.

The USA is an almost identical situation. At every level from the local under-7s to college campuses, soccer has the highest number of registered players. But at the top rung on the ladder, the professional (paid) players, the numbers fall away to nothing. The 'big four' – basketball, baseball, American football and ice hockey – monopolise TV, the sports pages, advertising, even the trading cards. There is simply no room for soccer.

Early days

Soccer was brought to Australia by English and Scottish immigrants in the mid-1880s. The first recorded soccer match in Australia took place in Sydney in 1880, between the Wanderers and Kings School. Wanderers won 5-0. The match was played at the Parramatta Common and drew a crowd of 1000.

From 1900 to the beginning of World War II in 1939, soccer steadily grew. It was especially popular in the New South Wales coalmining cities of Newcastle and Wollongong because there were so many British mine workers. These two areas produced more quality soccer players than the rest of the country put together.

After World War II, international Test series were

held with South Africa, New Zealand and Rhodesia. Then came the 1956 Olympics, which Melbourne hosted. Australia defeated Japan in the first round and went on to meet India for a place in the semi-finals. The Aussies started favourites and were beaten 4-2 in an upset. The final was watched by 90 000, the biggest-ever crowd for a sporting event in this country up to that time.

Although 1956 wasn't a winning year for Australia, a new and exciting era in Australian soccer was about to begin. Following World War II (1939-1945) huge numbers of Europeans left their war-torn homelands to start life again in countries like Australia. Migrants from countries like Italy, Greece, Holland, Austria and later in the 1950s Hungary, Czechoslovakia and Yugoslavia flocked to our shores. They brought with them their food, customs, beliefs and – of course – football.

As the influx of European players and fans grew from a trickle into a stream and then a wave, alarm bells began ringing. While many Australians welcomed the migrants, others did not. Soccer became 'the wog game' or 'wog ball' in some circles. Clubs that once had welcomed the arrival of a player trained in Europe now shut their doors.

Immigrants formed their own national sporting and social clubs, adding to the 'us and them' mentality. These new clubs were drawing crowds of 6000 or 7000 to their second-division matches – in contrast to many first-division Anglo-Australian clubs who were happy if 500 came along.

But although their standard of play was higher, these clubs couldn't get into first division – there was no promotion system. So they set up a breakaway NSW Soccer Federation. As it wasn't recognised by FIFA, the new Federation didn't have to abide by FIFA rules and could get players from other clubs without paying transfer fees. This was the pivotal moment in postwar Australian soccer. With the influx of central European footballers that followed there came a new and very different approach to the game. The British approach relied on strength, stamina and mental toughness. The Hungarian, Austrian and German teams put more emphasis on skill and tactics.

> **Soccer became 'the wog game' or 'wog ball' in some circles.**

The early 1960s saw the game flourish at club level as never before. In 1963 the Australian Soccer Federation was invited back into FIFA following its three-year suspension for 'irregularities' in the transfer of players (like not paying for them). The drawback was that domestic clubs could no longer import top-class European players because they could not afford the high transfer fees demanded.

In the early 1960s ABC-TV began televising 'Match of the Day' with Martin Royal. Shortly after this, live telecasts of the English Cup final began as well as weekly screenings of the top match from the English first division. Finally, in 1965, Australia played its first ever World Cup qualifying match. The venue was Phnom Penh, the opponent was North Korea. The result was two

losses 6-1 and 3-1, but that hardly mattered. Australia had arrived on the world stage.

A series of central European-born coaches began the task of shaping a national team with a distinctive and successful style. First there was Tiko Jelasevich, then in 1967 Joe Venglos, and finally 'Uncle Joe' Vlasits who was given the task of preparing Australia's 1970 World Cup challenge. After defeating Japan and South Korea the Aussies took on Rhodesia, then lost to the Israeli team. Israeli coach, E. Schaffer, commented, 'Physically and potentially, Australian soccer is better than ours. But tactically, they have a lot to learn'.

Finally, in 1974, under the guidance of coach Rale Razic, Australia qualified for the World Cup finals. First the Australian Socceroos had to overcome Iraq, Indonesia and New Zealand, which they did, not losing a single match of the six they played. Next came Iran, who were defeated 3-0 in Sydney. Despite losing the return match in Teheran 2-0, Australia still went to the next round on goal average.

The South Korean team came to Sydney and

> **Australia had arrived on the world stage.**

managed a goal-less draw. The second match in Seoul also ended in a draw, this time 2-2. A third game was played in Hong Kong three days later which Australia won 1-0 with perhaps the most famous goal in our history, Jimmy Mackay's 35-metre drive. Mackay's goal was considered to be of such quality that it was featured in the English TV show 'Big Match'. Truly a golden moment.

In the finals Australia was eliminated in the first round, following losses to East and West Germany and a draw with Chile. Still, our greatest result ever had been achieved.

In a display of genius found only in dictatorships and amateur sporting officials, the Australian Soccer Foundation decided that the fairest reward for this

THE HOLY GRAIL

Many people claim that soccer is treated like a religion. If this is true, then the holy grail of Australian soccer lies crumbling in a shoe box in Bondi Beach. The office belongs to Hakoah Soccer Club, the shoe box to Ms Sandra Ware and the boot to Jimmy Mackay. Yes indeed, folks, the very same Jimmy Mackay who with his 35-metre drive in the dying moments of the match sent Australia to the World Cup finals in West Germany in 1974. Australian soccer might be full of boots but there is only one we can call THE boot...this boot.

All hail
The Holy Grail
And Jimmy Mackay
Who did not fail.

achievement was to fire the man most responsible for it. Coach Razic was replaced by an Englishman, Frank Worthington. He was quickly replaced by Brian Green who was in turn replaced by Jim Shoulder. The national team lurched from crisis to crisis and was finally eliminated from the 1978 World Cup qualifiers by losing home and away games to Iran and Kuwait. This time the ASF in its wisdom did not replace the coach!

Australian soccer today

No team has yet managed to equal the achievements of Rale Razic and his band of part-timers. Their effort in getting into the 1974 World Cup finals is the high point of our soccer history. However, the 1990s have so far proved to be an optimistic and positive period. Our success in the Youth World Cup and the success of the Olyroos in qualifying for the last two Olympic tournaments have helped provide vital impetus for the sport.

> **No team has yet managed to equal the achievements of Rale Razic and his band of part-timers.**

A great addition to the Australian soccer landscape has been the SBS television and the familiar names of experts Les Murray and former Socceroo captain Johnny Warren. Since it began broadcasting in 1980, SBS has brought the best of world soccer into our lounge rooms every week.

Cable television will help soccer make a serious bid to become the number 1 sport at the professional level in this country. (Remember, it already is at every other level! – from under-5s to university.)

With Aussies enjoying unprecedented success in first-division European football, the whole sport is set for

---

DID YOU KNOW?

- The fastest goal in Australian soccer (or world soccer, for that matter) was scored by Adelaide player Damien Mori, in 3.6 seconds on 6 December 1995. Go, you little beauty!

---

its biggest boost in years. Players like Ned Zelic, Robbie Slater and Aurelio Vidmar are being joined by young guns like Paul Agostino, Mark Viduka, Zelco Kalac and Gabriel Mendez as regular faces on European TV.

Back home, players in the Ericsson Cup are enjoying bigger-than-ever coverage on SBS and the crowds at live matches are steadily building. The big question seems to be which step to take next. One popular idea is to establish a 'super league' involving clubs from Japan, Malaysia, Korea, the Pacific Islands and New Zealand. Another is to abandon the current national league and return to a strong state based competition similar to the 1960s and 1970s. Debate rages in clubs at all levels over which answer is the best one.

When I asked Johnny Warren about a national soccer identity, he said, 'Ideally the Australian style should be a beautiful blend of the English toughness and mental strength, the skills and technique of the central Europeans and Mediterraneans and the flamboyance of the Slavic and South Americans. Added to this would be the naturally aggressive style of Australians in sport...always taking the game to your opponents'.

The old idea of being valiant in defeat is just not good enough any more. The key to a better future for Australia in international football is believing that we *can* win against any opposition. And with the new wave of young Australians earning a living as full-time professional players around the world, we seem to be doing precisely that. (There are 80 Australian footballers playing with clubs overseas, including 31 in England, 10 in Malaysia and 4 in Hong Kong.)

Great moments: Zelic's ghosts, 1992

The Olyroos' path to the 1992 Olympic Games was always going to be tough – but when their final opponents were announced a lot of fans cancelled their holiday leave and cashed in their tickets for a refund. It was Holland, the outright favourite for the gold medal.

The first match was played in Sydney. It ended in a 1-1 draw, a noble result, a result one could be proud of.

The return match was in Rotterdam. The Dutch press laughed at the Australians. When the Aussies said publicly that they expected to win, the laughs turned to howls of derision. Then came the day of the final.

The Australians, led by Robbie Slater, attacked the Dutch like a white pointer in a feeding frenzy. Finally sweeper Ned Zelic slipped unseen ('ghosted') into the penalty area just before half time and scored. The Dutch

---

DID YOU KNOW?

- The record transfer fee for an Australian was paid for Aurelio Vidmar when he moved from Standard to Feyenoord in June 1995. The fee was $5.2 million.
- The record fee for a transfer from Australia is $1.7 million. It was paid for Zelco Kalac to go from Sydney United to Leicester in July 1995.

fought back with great character in the second half and levelled the scores. The Aussies looked tired, defeated.

They were into extra time, and the Dutch scored again. Surely this was the match. The Australians had been magnificent but it looked as though they had battled themselves to a standstill.

> **The Australians attacked the Dutch like a white pointer in a feeding frenzy.**

Then, with only a minute or so remaining, Zelic again ghosted into the attack, ran 50 metres and then, from an impossible angle on the right, beat the keeper with a shot that will surely live on in the memory of those who saw it.

Ray Baartz's story

Saturday 27 April 1974 should have gone down as one of the most significant dates in Australian soccer history. But for Ray Baartz, Australia's star striker, it turned into a nightmare he will never forget.

The Socceroos were to play two warm-up matches against Uruguay as part of their preparation for the World Cup final. It was the fifth World Cup the Uruguayans had qualified for (they'd won it twice). They were considered a major force in South American football.

The first match in Melbourne ended in a 0-0 draw – a result beyond most Australian soccer fans' wildest dreams. For the Uruguayans, it was a disgrace. (Remember that in 1974 Australia was a nobody in world football.)

The second match, three days later at Sydney, was Uruguay's chance for revenge. But the Socceroos had other ideas. It was a brutal game, played as hard as any

World Cup tie. With tension building, Ray Baartz scored, giving Australia a 1-0 lead. Trapping a pass 20 metres out, he steadied himself and then cannoned his shot into the top of the net.

All hell broke loose. Socceroos began dropping like ninepins beneath vicious and repeated fouling. Uruguay equalised but the referee disallowed the goal as a hand ball. Then, behind the play, Uruguayan defender Louis Garisto karate-chopped Ray Baartz in the back of the neck. Baartz collapsed. The linesman reported the foul but Garisto refused to leave the ground for five minutes. Finally he was escorted off the ground, with the crowd screaming for blood as Baartz, still on the ground, was treated by medicos. Finally Baartz regained his feet and the game went on. The Uruguayans attacked with everything they had, but the Socceroos refused to crack. Then with five minutes remaining, Baartz pounced on a loose ball and found big Peter Ollerton with his pass. Ollerton raced 40 metres, swept past the goalkeeper and scored. 2-0 Australia!

At first, soccer media around the world refused to believe that Australia could have beaten Uruguay. United Press International (UPI) checked the score seven times before they would believe it!

Later, in the dressing room, Ray Baartz collapsed again and was later ruled unfit to play in the World Cup final. A devastating and tragic blow. It was the end of his first-class career.

6 Fans

'Football is about playing for the fans, about pleasing them...' Johan Cruyff, 1990.

'That's right.' Damien Lovelock, 1996.

Fans come in all shapes and sizes and for more reasons than there are minutes in a day. The spectacle of 50 000 or more spectators watching two world-class sides on the lush green playing surface is awesome, whether it's under brilliant sunshine or the dazzle of floodlights. The passion, the drama, the tension, the euphoria – it's a great argument for sport.

Psychologists, sociologists, social anthropologists, psychiatrists and my mother have wondered why sports fans behave as they do. Some say tribalism, others the need to belong, still others that it's part of an instinct for warfare and survival. Karl Marx said it was a trick used by the ruling class to keep the workers busy and so avoid a working class revolution. My mother said it's because most men are idiots who never grow up and like to play in the mud or watch others play in the mud. Take your pick.

My own response to the question 'Why are you so keen on soccer?' is to recall certain favourite moments from my memory bank. Watching Ray Baartz blast a free kick past Lev Yashin, possibly the world's greatest goalkeeper, from 35 metres out (Sydney, around 1970). Listening to Les Murray call Charlie Yanko's 50-metre free

kick against Israel.
Watching Ned Zelic
score two of the greatest
goals by any Australian
player in the most
dramatic of
circumstances to send
Australia to the Olympic
finals (Rotterdam, 1992).
Watching the Republic
of Ireland defeat
England in the 1988
European Champion-
ships for the first time in
2500 years (or very
nearly). Watching my
son's team in his first
year in soccer draw a grand final against a team that had
beaten them 6-0, 5-0 and 4-0 earlier that year.

So, do you understand now why people become
fans? If you are one yourself then you already know, and
if you're not...try it, you might just find it's for you. One
thing is for sure, it'd be a different game without them.

Riot and mayhem: how does it happen?

Soccer madness takes many forms. I love the game itself
for its own sake, but others care only about a particular
team. Unfortunately this seems to mean that you have to
hate every other team and player to demonstrate the depth
of your devotion as a fan. The worst example of this was
probably the Heysel Stadium collapse in Brussels on 29
May 1985. Liverpool and Juventus fans rioted and caused a

DID YOU KNOW?

• On 28 June 1969, Honduras and El Salvador met in a World Cup qualifying match in Mexico City, won 3-2 by El Salvador in extra time. Following this, El Salvador invaded Honduras, sparking a three-day war in which more than 3000 people were killed.

---

wall to collapse. Thirty-eight people were crushed. And the TV cameras were there – it was all recorded.

Endless theories have been put forward to explain this disaster in particular and football hooliganism in general. The answer? They just don't know.

Crowding maybe has something to do with it (and alcohol). If too many people are packed into too-small stadiums, they can get aggressive or panicky. (And why are too many people allowed in? Money. It bumps up ticket sales.)

Sometimes disaster happens because officials have locked the exits to prevent gatecrashers getting in – and then people inside can't get out in a hurry when they need to. This happened in the Bradford fire, also in 1985, when 57 people died.

Whatever your theory, it has to be said that 99 per cent of the fans are ordinary, peaceable people who know it's only a game.

The tragic tale of Andreas Escobar

When the 1994 World Cup finals began in the USA, many people thought the Colombians had the strongest chance. Earlier in 1994 they had trounced Argentina 5-0 – the biggest defeat in Argentina's history – and qualified for the finals. Then Colombia lost 3-1 to Romania – that meant they had to win the next match. To make the pressure even greater, the families of the coach and some players had been threatened with death, unless certain changes were made to the team. The coach reluctantly went along with the demands. On top of this the Colombians were to play the host team, USA, which had the support of 270 million fellow Americans. It was pressure heaped on pressure.

The Colombians began well, but then began to seem hesitant – they lost the attacking flow that was their trademark. After 35 minutes, the US hit a cross into the Colombian penalty area. Defender Andreas Escobar lunged at the ball, deflecting it past the Colombian goalkeeper and into his own net. The US scored again and it was only in the last minute of the game that Colombia finally found the net. It was too little, too late: USA won 2-1.

Six days later Andreas Escobar was at a restaurant with his wife when two drunk men began abusing him. After a heated argument, Escobar and his wife left. The two men followed and in a fit of drunken rage shot and killed Andreas Escobar. Their reason? They had bet some money on the game and blamed Escobar for their (not very large) financial loss. A sad and shameful episode in World Cup history.

DID YOU KNOW?
- The record attendance for a football match is 205,000 which was set at the Maracana Stadium in Rio de Janeiro on 16 July 1950. Brazil lost 2-1 to Uruguay.

7 The money factor: professionalism

Today's footballers, in the big clubs and at national/international level, are professionals – they are paid to play. Soccer is their job. It wasn't always like that – in the olden days it was a spare-time hobby.

The rise of soccer as a professional sport really started in the 1950s in Europe. Many people welcomed it as a 'good thing' because it allowed players to concentrate exclusively on the game. By the 1960s the top players in European football were beginning to earn serious money.

George Best was a great example. At his peak he earned more than the Prime Minister and most top businessmen. How? Endorsements. Best's playing wages were only a tiny fraction of his wealth. The rest came from advertising eggs, milk, football boots, cars, holidays in

Spain, etc., etc. Why? Television. Televised sport proved to be the most astonishing success story of the entertainment industry. Look at Michael Jordan and Gatorade, Shane Warne and Nike.

The 1970s saw a massive change in the way football was structured. Once the companies realised the potential for advertising through sport the money simply poured in from everywhere. Basically this is what happened:

1 Football clubs needed to be successful to attract sponsorship and advertising.

2 To be successful they needed top-class players.

3 This cost an absolute fortune.

4 To get the necessary cash, clubs began to sign huge endorsement deals with multi-national corporations, effectively becoming part of the corporation themselves. For example, teams like Juventus, Inter Milan and AC Milan in Italy's industrial north became entirely funded by giant corporations like Fiat, sometimes to the tune of $100 million or more.

Winning teams were on TV all the time. Great. The trouble was that there has always been a limited supply of brilliant attacking players, so you couldn't always guarantee your sponsor a win. However, not losing, that was another matter entirely. Defensive soccer, defensive tactics, defensive coaching became all the rage, as we saw in Chapter 3.

By the 1980s things had got so out of hand that the average first-division Italian match actually consisted of less than 45 minutes playing time! The rest was spent with endless free kicks from repetitive fouling, time-wasting by goalkeepers and players taking throw-ins and

DID YOU KNOW?

- The best goalkeeper ever was Dino Zoff of Italy who kept a clean sheet for 1142 minutes between September 1972 and June 1974.

free kicks, or diving by forwards to attract unjustified free kicks and penalties. It was a shameful disgrace, caused largely by the corporatisation of football.

In the 1990s FIFA has finally seen the light and begun making changes to bring back the 'beautiful

game'. No backpassing to goalkeepers, red cards for a professional foul, yellow cards for time-wasting and diving. These changes are long overdue.

Meanwhile the money keeps rolling in. Some estimates put football as a $300-billion a year industry. Not bad for kicking a ball around a park. As the old song says, 'nice work if you can get it.' You betcha!

8 Women's soccer

Ten years ago, describing the position of women's soccer in the overall game would have been a fairly easy task... invisible, non-existent, etc. Happily, this is no longer the case. Since the second women's World Cup, won by the amateurs Norway who defeated the virtually full-time professional USA, women's football has had a tremendous groundswell of growth and support.

But women's soccer isn't new. In England women's football matches date back to at least 1895. During World War I (1914–18) it really got going, and on Boxing Day

1920, 53 000 people turned up to watch a match at Goodison Park. In 1921 the English FA concluded that the women's game was becoming a threat to 'the game in general' (meaning the men's game), and so women's football was banned for 50 years.

81

> **...women's football was banned for 50 years**

This was par for the course then. Even now sportswomen have to contend with gender bias, shown in lack of sponsorship and media coverage and poor access to proper facilities. But things are changing, slowly.

Today very successful competitions are running in the Scandinavian countries (Denmark, Norway, Sweden and Finland) as well as West Germany and Italy (who both have semi-professional competitions) and Britain (which is attempting to recapture its past glory days). In the United States the college-based circuit is flourishing and top players can make a good living in product endorsements (advertisements). Surprise, surprise, Japan has a full-time professional league already. Things are happening in Africa, Asia and Oceania.

The key moment in women's soccer would undoubtedly be the first women's World Cup, held in the People's Republic of China in 1991 and won by the United States. This legitimised the sport and has allowed it to develop in leaps and bounds since. With clear and focused administration, the sky is the limit for the biggest growth area in modern soccer.

DID YOU KNOW?
- There are over 150 million registered FIFA participants world wide, and 10 million of these are women.
- Adidas is planning to release a soccer boot designed specifically for women in 1996. You've really made it when you've got your own boot.

9 Dream teams

If you could choose any player from any time, what would be your all-time best team? Here's my choice of players for the best ever Australian side. I asked SBS soccer experts Les Murray and Lou Gautier to list their teams as well.

Damien's Australian XI

BOSNICH (goalkeeper)   Gets the nod because he's proved himself on the world stage. Has a fantastic career ahead of him.

DAVIDSON (right back)   Terrific workrate. Classic overlapping fullback. Gets there just ahead of Utjesenovic.

SCHAEFER (centre back) The rock of St George and Australia in the 1960s and 1970s. Unforgiving defender of 'the old school'.

WATKISS (centre back) Beautiful stylist. A complete player and perfect foil for Schaefer. Useful in attack as well.

WILLIAMS (left back) Gets in ahead of

Curran and Tony Vidmar. Solid in defence and lethal on the overlap.

ZELIC (centre midfield)   Scorer of *that* goal for the Olyroos in their 1992 qualifier in Rotterdam. Has been compared to the great Franz Beckenbauer. There can be no higher praise.

SLATER (right wing)   Explosive runner and striker of the ball. Was a great favourite in France. Played with English champions Blackburn and now West Ham.

WARREN (deep centre forward)   Perhaps Australia's greatest all-round player. Inspired the wonderful Socceroos to reach West Germany in 1974.

BAARTZ (left half wing)   One of the most powerful strikers ever produced in Australia. Scored a bundle of outrageous goals for Hakoah, New South Wales, and Australia. Tragically his career was cut short at its pinnacle by a Uruguyan defender in Sydney in 1974. Was sorely missed at the World Cup finals in West Germany.

ABONYI (striker)   Beautifully balanced forward for St George in 1960s and 1970s.

KRNCEVIC (striker) Although he had a limited
representative career, Eddie blazed the trail into
Belgian first-division football and top-scored there.
Masterful in the 18 yard box.

RESERVES: Crino (midfield) Vidmar (forward)
Both creative and able to turn a game.

Lou Gautier's Australian XI

MARK BOSNICH Despite his youth (he's only 23), he is
already the best goalkeeper Australia has ever
produced – and we have produced our fair share of top
keepers. After two seasons at Manchester United, he
has emerged as one of the world's top goalies at
Aston Villa.

DOUG UTJESENOVIC Brilliant attacking fullback for
St George and a key member of the 1974 Socceroos.
One of the first attacking fullbacks in Australian
football.

MILAN IVANOVIC This naturalised former Yugoslav is a
mainstay of Adelaide City and Australia, despite his 34
years. His silky skills and cool head stamp him as
Australia's best *libero*.

MANFRED SCHAEFER The best stopper of the late 1960s and
mid-1970s, his match-winning performances for St
George and Australia stamp him as our very top
stopper of all time.

TONY VIDMAR An attacking fullback who has shown his
class at Adelaide City and with the Socceroos after a
brilliant display at the 1992 Olympics.

JOHN WARREN The best-known and most respected
former player in Australia, Warren was the very soul

of St George and Australia from the mid-1960s to early 1970s. A shining example in any midfield, he was unsurpassed as an inspirational onfield leader.

NED ZELIC   Caught the country's imagination with the two goals that qualified the Olyroos for Barcelona. Has performed well in the midfield and at *libero* since being transferred to Germany, despite injuries.

PAUL OKON   The best young Socceroo at Portugal 1991. Okon has rated among the top three players in the Belgium first division since joining FC Bruges. His onfield vision and positioning stamp him as the best *libero* born in Australia.

AURELIO VIDMAR   Won the Belgian first-division goal-scoring crown this season – the third Australian to do so. His brilliant performances for the Socceroos in the 1993 World Cup qualifiers earned him Oceania Player of the Year honours. In my book, the best Aussie playing the game today.

EDDIE KRNCEVIC   Left Australia at an early age to play professional football in Europe. He emerged as one of that continent's most feared strikers during his spell at Anderlecht, when he won the Belgian goal-scoring title. One of the best-known Australian soccer players in Europe.

FRANK FARINA   Like Vidmar and Krncevic, Farina topped the Belgian first division goal-scoring. Dominated the NSL scoring charts before he joined Club Bruges in 1988.

RESERVES: Robbie Slater, Atti Abonyi   Slater was voted Oceania Player of the Year in 1993 for his world-class displays against Argentina. He was the idol of Lens fans in France before moving to Blackburn, the

English champions. A midfield dynamo who never stops running. Abonyi was the classiest striker of the 1960s and 1970s. A ball-player who scored goals for both St George and the Socceroos. Our best player at the 1974 World Cup finals.

COACH: Eddie Thomson Love him or hate him, Thomson has done the job. He coached the all-conquering Sydney City team in all its pre-1987 NSL triumphs, and took the Olyroos to the semi-finals of the 1992 Olympics.

Les Murray's Australian XI

BOSNICH	TONY VIDMAR	WARREN
SCHAEFER	CRINO	ABONYI
WATKISS	SLATER	AURELIO VIDMAR
DAVIDSON	ZELIC	

RESERVES: Baartz and Okon
COACH: Frank Arok

We also chose a best-ever world team each. Here they are.

Damien's world XI

LEV YASHIN (goalkeeper) USSR Yashin or Banks: Banks or Yashin. In the end I'd take Yashin for his height.

FRANZ BECKENBAUER (*libero*) Germany One of the best players of his era and definitely the player against which all *libero*s are measured. In a class of his own.

ALBERTO (right back) Brazil
One of the two players to
define the role of the
overlapping fullback.
Scored one of the great
World Cup goals in the
1970 final against Italy.

GENTILE (centre back) Italy
A man who carried a
well-deserved reputation
as a hard man. However,
at man-to-man marking
he was the best.
Absolutely unshakable.
Starred in Italy's 1982
campaign.

FACCHETTI (left back) Italy   The only good thing to come
out of *Catenaccio*. Elegant in both attack and defence.
The prototype for Maldini and countless others.

CRUYFF (midfield) Holland   The wonderkid. Explosive
pace, outstanding vision and mobility. The
orchestrator of total football. The genius of the 1970s.

PELÉ (right midfield) Brazil   Possibly the greatest
footballer of all time. A lethal striker and a great
provider.

MARADONA (left midfield) Argentina   Playing behind Van
Basten and Eusebio, he would punish any defence
with his passing and his runs. Scorer of arguably the
greatest goal in World Cup history against England in
1986.

GEORGE BEST (right wing) Northern Ireland   His dribbling
skills were beyond belief. Like Cruyff, his career was

cut short. The greatest player to never play a World Cup final series.

MARCO VAN BASTEN (striker) Holland   Magnificent if somewhat erratic goal-scorer. Ruled the roost in Italy's club competition at its peak. Troubled by severe ankle injuries. His goal in the European championship win in 1988 had to be seen to be believed.

EUSEBIO (left wing) Portugal   Tremendous pace and skill combined with an unbelievably explosive left-foot shot.

RESERVES: Platini France, Rijkaard Holland   Between them they could cover any position on the field.

Lou Gautier's world XI

SEPP MAIER   I picked him ahead of Gordon Banks because of his three dominant performances when his club side, Bayern Munich, won the European Champions Cup in 1974 and 1976 and Germany the 1974 World Cup.

GIACINTO FACCHETTI   Was the dominant fullback in Europe with Inter Milan when the club dominated European football in the mid-1960s. I picked him ahead of Karl-Heinz Schnellinger of Germany.

ELIAS FIGUEROA   Voted South American Player of the Year no less than five times in the 1970s. This Chilean maestro was a vintage sweeper who had no peer.

FRANZ BECKENBAUER   Revolutionised the *libero* role and dominated his position for more than a decade (1966-78). Won countless honours for his club Bayern Munich, and for Germany.

PAOLO MALDINI   His father, Cesare Maldini, was another Italian international defender. Paolo is regarded as the best fullback of his generation. Since emerging in 1988 he has been a star for both AC Milan and Italy.

BOBBY CHARLTON   The best English soccer player of his generation. Charlton played a major part in England's 1966 World Cup victory, and in Manchester United's 1968 European Champions Cup triumph. Brilliant at tactics, he was also one of the world game's fairest players.

MICHEL PLATINI   The mastermind of the French and Juventus midfield from 1977 to 1986, the little Frenchman made and scored goals. Free kicks from any distance or angle were a speciality.

JOHAN CRUYFF   He was total football's shining light, the inspiration behind Holland. He led Holland to the 1974 and 1978 World Cup finals, and Ajax Amsterdam (which he also captained) to three straight European Champions Cups in the early 1970s.

DIEGO MARADONA   El Pibo d'Oro (the Golden Child) burst on the world scene at the Under 20 World Cup in Tunisia and held centre stage until bowing out in disgrace from USA in 1994. An incomparable dribbler, he led Argentina to one World Cup title and his Italian club Napoli to Italian and European honours.

PELÉ   The best player that ever lived – a legend in his own lifetime. Burst on the scene as a match-winner in the 1958 World Cup at age 17 – and never looked back. Scored 1300+ goals in a career during which he only served two clubs – Santos and the New York Cosmos. Voted 'Sportsman of the 20th Century'.

GEORGE BEST   The enfant terrible of British football enchanted an entire generation (1966-1974) with his silky skills. On his day, none was better than the Manchester United winger, but this flawed genius' career ended far too early.

RESERVES: Zico, Gerd Muller   'The White Zico' played until 1994, when he was 36 years old. A brilliant midfielder-cum-striker, he featured in top-class football for 15 years. Muller was the heart and soul of the German and Bayern Munich attack for more than a decade. This goal-scorer extraordinaire scored 14 World Cup goals – a record that may stand forever.

COACH: Happel   The greatest player produced by Austrian football won five European Cups with five different clubs and also steered eight different club sides to victory.

Les Murray's world XI

GORDON BANKS (goal)   It wasn't just his miracle save against Pelé in Mexico 1970. Banks was the perfect all-round keeper: he had superb reflexes, agility, bravery, positional sense. He was acrobatic enough to be flashy when necessary, but was never reckless.

FRANZ BECKENBAUER (*libero*)   The model of the technically complete, creative sweeper. Der Kaiser was a player of supreme intelligence and vision, not to mention perfect ball control. He was the first of the 'offensive' sweepers, one who probes forward, creating an extra midfielder and a crucial numerical advantage.

FRANCO BARESI (centre back) Perhaps the most professional, intelligent and cunning centre back of them all, for over a decade. A marvellous reader of the game and the prefect rearguard organiser, so vital in a zonal defence. Also excellent going forward, his forays always exquisitely timed.

PAUL BREITNER (right back), PAOLO MALDINI (left back) Both are selected for their fine attacking tendencies and abilities from defensive positions. Even though Breitner was a left back with club and country, he was two-footed and would slot in well on the right. In my team I would expect both to assault the opposition with a high frequency of overlap runs, something they were both brilliant at.

SOCRATES (deep central midfield) The great Brazilian, a real general, would suit as the prompter from a deep position, able to join in the assault on goal when it's on. He was a superbly intelligent passer with marvellous vision, but also brilliant at getting into the box for scoring positions.

JOHAN CRUYFF and MICHEL PLATINI (right and left midfield) The two flankers in a diamond-shaped midfield, these two men are universally known for their vision, brilliance in taking defenders on and, especially in Cruyff's case, explosive pace with the ball.

DIEGO MARADONA (attacking midfield or *mezza punta*)
No need to describe his fantastic abilities. Playing in
the 'hole' just behind the strikers is Maradona's
natural role. I would also make him captain for, apart
from Baresi, he has no rival in this team for
leadership qualities.

GEORGE BEST (flank striker)   George's all-round genius
was always best used on the flank, but there has
never been a more versatile winger. In my team Best
would switch from flank to flank, as needed. His wing
play would create the room for others to exploit
central scoring positions.

PELÉ (striker)   Mine is a versatile team, playing in a
'whirl' not unlike the great Dutch teams. So having
Pelé as striker does not mean he would be
permanently buried in a crowd of defenders in the
opposing box. He would switch and interchange just
like all the others, but because of his unrivalled
qualities as a finisher, with head and both feet, his
primary task would be to score goals.

RESERVES: Zico and Marco van Basten

COACH: Rinus Michels   Like all coaches, Michels has had
his failures. But for sheer inventiveness, his major
role in fashioning 'total football', he is the only man
who could coach this team.

10 World Cup winners

Date	Played at	
1930	Uruguay	Uruguay won 4-2 against Argentina
1934	Italy	Italy won 2-0 against Czechoslovakia
1938	France	Italy won 4-2 against Hungary
1950	Brazil	Uruguay won 2-1 against Brazil
1954	Switzerland	Germany won 3-2 against Hungary
1958	Sweden	Brazil won 5-2 against Sweden
1962	Chile	Brazil won 3-1 against Czechoslovakia
1966	England	England won 4-2 against West Germany
1970	Mexico	Brazil won 4-1 against Italy
1974	West Germany	West Germany won 2-1 against the Netherlands [Holland]
1978	Argentina	Argentina won 3-1 against the Netherlands
1982	Spain	Italy won 3-1 against West Germany
1986	Mexico	Argentina won 3-2 against West Germany
1990	Italy	West Germany won 1-0 against Argentina
1994	USA	Brazil won 0-0 (on penalties) against Italy

Further reading (and viewing)

Encyclopedia of Australian Soccer 1922-88
Showcase Publications, 1988

Rothmans' Encyclopedia of World Football
W.H. Smith, 1990

The Simplest Game
Collier Books, 1994

The Story of Football
by Martin Tyler
Marshall Cavendish Books, 1978

Most of the great soccer books go out of print very
quickly. It's worth looking in second-hand bookshops,
where you can sometimes pick up gems like Johnny
Warren's *Soccer of Australia* for a few dollars. Or you can
contact your local soccer federation.

Videos

Soccer videos are easy to find. Two of the best are
The History of Soccer, put out by Transworld, and
The 100 Greatest Goals, volume 1, put out by Virgin,
which includes rare footage of Johan Cruyff in action.

For other suggestions, contact the experts at SBS
television.

Index